THESE BREWS BELONG TO:

_____

BREW #1

Name your brew!

_____

_____

_____

BREW #1:

DATE: _____

BREW GOAL

_____

_____

_____

_____

BREW SIZE

_____

INGREDIENTS

GRAINS

HOPS   YEAST

EXTRACT Y / N

BREW #1:

GRAVITY READINGS

ORIGINAL GRAVITY (OG)

FINAL GRAVITY (FG)

ALCOHOL BY VOLUME (ABV)

INTERNATIONAL BITTERNESS UNITS (IBUs):

TEMPERATURE READINGS

PROCESS FOLLOWED

BREW #1: _____

_____
_____
_____

RESULTS

FLAVORS   SMELL   COLOR

CLARITY | HEAD | STRENGTH | FINISH

WHO TRIED IT? WHAT FEEDBACK DID YOU GET?

_____
_____
_____

WHAT ADJUSTMENTS WOULD YOU MAKE NEXT TIME?

_____
_____
_____

BREW #2

Name your brew!

_____

_____

_____

BREW #2: _____

BREW GOAL

_____
_____
_____
_____

BREW SIZE

_____

INGREDIENTS

GRAINS

HOPS   YEAST

EXTRACT Y / N

BREW #2:

ORIGINAL GRAVITY (OG)

FINAL GRAVITY (FG)

ALCOHOL BY VOLUME (ABV)

INTERNATIONAL BITTERNESS UNITS (IBUs):

TEMPERATURE READINGS

PROCESS FOLLOWED

BREW #2:

RESULTS

FLAVORS   SMELL   COLOR

CLARITY | HEAD | STRENGTH | FINISH

WHO TRIED IT? WHAT FEEDBACK DID YOU GET?

WHAT ADJUSTMENTS WOULD YOU MAKE NEXT TIME?

BREW #3

Name your brew!

_____

_____

_____

BREW #3:

BREW GOAL

BREW SIZE

INGREDIENTS

GRAINS

HOPS   YEAST

EXTRACT   Y / N

BREW #3:

GRAVITY READINGS

ORIGINAL GRAVITY
(OG)

FINAL GRAVITY
(FG)

ALCOHOL BY
VOLUME (ABV)

INTERNATIONAL BITTERNESS UNITS (IBUs):

TEMPERATURE READINGS

PROCESS FOLLOWED

BREW #3:

_____

_____

_____

RESULTS

FLAVORS   SMELL   COLOR

CLARITY | HEAD | STRENGTH | FINISH

WHO TRIED IT? WHAT FEEDBACK DID YOU GET?

_____

_____

_____

WHAT ADJUSTMENTS WOULD YOU MAKE NEXT TIME?

_____

_____

_____

BREW #4

Name your brew!

_____

_____

_____

BREW #4:

DATE: _____

BREW GOAL

_____

_____

_____

_____

BREW SIZE

_____

INGREDIENTS

GRAINS

HOPS   YEAST

EXTRACT   Y / N

BREW #4:

GRAVITY READINGS

ORIGINAL GRAVITY (OG)	FINAL GRAVITY (FG)	ALCOHOL BY VOLUME (ABV)

INTERNATIONAL BITTERNESS UNITS (IBUs):

TEMPERATURE READINGS

_____

_____

_____

PROCESS FOLLOWED

_____

_____

_____

_____

_____

_____

_____

_____

_____

_____

BREW #4:

RESULTS

FLAVORS   SMELL   COLOR

CLARITY   HEAD   STRENGTH   FINISH

WHO TRIED IT? WHAT FEEDBACK DID YOU GET?

WHAT ADJUSTMENTS WOULD YOU MAKE NEXT TIME?

BREW #5

Name your brew!

_____

_____

_____

BREW #5:

BREW GOAL

_____

_____

_____

_____

BREW SIZE

_____

INGREDIENTS

GRAINS

HOPS   YEAST

EXTRACT Y / N

BREW #5:

GRAVITY READINGS

ORIGINAL GRAVITY (OG)

FINAL GRAVITY (FG)

ALCOHOL BY VOLUME (ABV)

INTERNATIONAL BITTERNESS UNITS (IBUs):

TEMPERATURE READINGS

PROCESS FOLLOWED

BREW #5:

FIRST IMPRESSION

RESULTS

FLAVORS   SMELL   COLOR

CLARITY | HEAD | STRENGTH | FINISH

WHO TRIED IT? WHAT FEEDBACK DID YOU GET?

WHAT ADJUSTMENTS WOULD YOU MAKE NEXT TIME?

BREW #6

Name your brew!

_____

_____

_____

BREW #6:

BREW GOAL

_____

_____

_____

_____

BREW SIZE

_____

INGREDIENTS

GRAINS

HOPS   YEAST

EXTRACT Y / N

BREW #6:

GRAVITY READINGS

ORIGINAL GRAVITY (OG)	FINAL GRAVITY (FG)	ALCOHOL BY VOLUME (ABV)

INTERNATIONAL BITTERNESS UNITS (IBUs):

TEMPERATURE READINGS

_____

_____

_____

PROCESS FOLLOWED

_____

_____

_____

_____

_____

_____

_____

_____

_____

_____

BREW #6:

FIRST IMPRESSION

_____

_____

_____

RESULTS

FLAVORS   SMELL   COLOR

CLARITY | HEAD | STRENGTH | FINISH

WHO TRIED IT? WHAT FEEDBACK DID YOU GET?

_____

_____

_____

WHAT ADJUSTMENTS WOULD YOU MAKE NEXT TIME?

_____

_____

_____

BREW #7

Name your brew!

_____

_____

_____

BREW #7:

DATE: _____

BREW GOAL

_____
_____
_____
_____

BREW SIZE

_____

INGREDIENTS

GRAINS

HOPS   YEAST

EXTRACT Y / N

BREW #7:

GRAVITY READINGS

ORIGINAL GRAVITY
(OG)

FINAL GRAVITY
(FG)

ALCOHOL BY
VOLUME (ABV)

INTERNATIONAL BITTERNESS UNITS (IBUs):

TEMPERATURE READINGS

_____

_____

_____

PROCESS FOLLOWED

_____

_____

_____

_____

_____

_____

_____

_____

_____

_____

BREW #7:

FIRST IMPRESSION

RESULTS

FLAVORS   SMELL   COLOR

CLARITY | HEAD | STRENGTH | FINISH

WHO TRIED IT? WHAT FEEDBACK DID YOU GET?

WHAT ADJUSTMENTS WOULD YOU MAKE NEXT TIME?

BREW #8

Name your brew!

_____

_____

_____

BREW #8:

DATE: _____

BREW GOAL

_____

_____

_____

_____

BREW SIZE

_____

INGREDIENTS

GRAINS

HOPS   YEAST

EXTRACT   Y / N

BREW #8:

GRAVITY READINGS

ORIGINAL GRAVITY (OG)	FINAL GRAVITY (FG)	ALCOHOL BY VOLUME (ABV)

INTERNATIONAL BITTERNESS UNITS (IBUs):

TEMPERATURE READINGS

PROCESS FOLLOWED

BREW #8:

RESULTS

FLAVORS   SMELL   COLOR

CLARITY | HEAD | STRENGTH | FINISH

WHO TRIED IT? WHAT FEEDBACK DID YOU GET?

WHAT ADJUSTMENTS WOULD YOU MAKE NEXT TIME?

BREW #9

Name your brew!

_____

_____

_____

BREW #9:

DATE: _____

BREW GOAL

_____
_____
_____
_____

BREW SIZE

_____

INGREDIENTS

GRAINS

HOPS

YEAST

EXTRACT   Y / N

BREW #9:

GRAVITY READINGS

ORIGINAL GRAVITY (OG)   FINAL GRAVITY (FG)   ALCOHOL BY VOLUME (ABV)

INTERNATIONAL BITTERNESS UNITS (IBUs):

TEMPERATURE READINGS

PROCESS FOLLOWED

BREW #9:

RESULTS

FLAVORS   SMELL   COLOR

CLARITY | HEAD | STRENGTH | FINISH

WHO TRIED IT? WHAT FEEDBACK DID YOU GET?

WHAT ADJUSTMENTS WOULD YOU MAKE NEXT TIME?

BREW #10

Name your brew!

_____

_____

_____

BREW #10:

DATE: _____

BREW GOAL

_____
_____
_____
_____

BREW SIZE

_____

INGREDIENTS

GRAINS

HOPS   YEAST

EXTRACT Y / N

BREW #10:

GRAVITY READINGS

ORIGINAL GRAVITY
(OG)

FINAL GRAVITY
(FG)

ALCOHOL BY
VOLUME (ABV)

INTERNATIONAL BITTERNESS UNITS (IBUs):

TEMPERATURE READINGS

PROCESS FOLLOWED

BREW #10: _____

_____
_____
_____

RESULTS

FLAVORS   SMELL   COLOR

CLARITY | HEAD | STRENGTH | FINISH

WHO TRIED IT? WHAT FEEDBACK DID YOU GET?

_____
_____
_____

WHAT ADJUSTMENTS WOULD YOU MAKE NEXT TIME?

_____
_____
_____

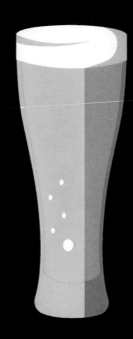

24 HOURS IN A DAY, 24 BEERS IN A CASE. COINCIDENCE?

- Stephen Wright